ASSURANCE

ASSURANCE

J C Ryle

Christian Focus Publications

©1992 Christian Focus Publications

ISBN 1 871 676 0 53

Published by
Christian Focus Publications Ltd
Geanies House, Fearn, Ross-shire,
IV20 1TW, Scotland, Great Britain.

Cover design
by
Seoris N. McGillivray.

Printed and bound in Great Britain by
Cox & Wyman Ltd, Reading

Contents

INTRODUCTION

I am now ready to be offered, and the time of my departure is at hand. I have fought a good fight, I have finished my course, I have kept the faith: henceforth there is laid up for me a crown of righteousness, which the Lord, the righteous judge, shall give me at that day: And not to me only, but unto all them also that love his appearing (2 Tim 4:6, 7, 8).

Reader,
In the words of Scripture which head this page, you see the

Apostle Paul looking three ways: downward, backward, forward. Downward to the grave, - backward to his own ministry, - forward to that great day, the day of judgment.

I invite you this day to stand by the Apostle's side a few minutes, and mark the words he uses. Happy is that soul who can look where Paul looked, and then speak as Paul spoke!

He looks *downward* to the grave, and he does it without fear. Hear what he says. 'I am ready to be offered.' I am like an animal brought to the place of sacrifice, and bound with cords to the very horns of the altar. The wine and oil have been poured on my head, according to the custom. The last ceremonies have been gone through. Every preparation has been made. It only remains to receive the death-blow, and then all is over.

'The time of my departure is at hand.' I am like a ship about to unmoor and put to sea. All on board is ready. I only wait to have the moorings cast off that fasten me to the shore, and I shall then set sail and begin my voyage.

Reader, these are glorious words to come from the lips of a child of Adam like ourselves. Death is a solemn thing, and never so much so as when we see it close at hand.

The grave is a chilling, heart-sickening place, and it is vain to pretend it has no terrors. Yet here is a mortal man who can look calmly into the narrow house appointed for all living, and say, while he stands upon the brink, 'I see it all, and am not afraid.'

Let us listen to him again. He looks *backward* to his ministerial life, and he does it without shame. Hear what he says. 'I have fought the good fight.' There he speaks as a soldier. I have fought that good battle with the world, the flesh and the devil, from which so many shrink and draw back.

'I have finished my course.' There he speaks as one who has

run for a prize. I have run the race marked out for me: I have gone over the ground appointed for me, however rough and steep. I have not turned aside because of difficulties, nor been discouraged by the length of the way. I am at last in sight of the goal.

'I have kept the faith.' There he speaks as a steward. I have held fast that glorious Gospel which was committed to my trust. I have not mingled it with man's traditions, nor spoiled its simplicity by adding my own inventions, nor allowed others to adulterate it without withstanding them to the face. 'As a soldier, - a runner, - a steward,' he seems to say, 'I am not ashamed.'

Reader, that Christian his happy who, as he quits this world, can leave such testimony behind him. A good conscience will save no man, - wash away no sin, - nor lift us one hair's breadth toward heaven. Yet, a good conscience will be found a pleasant visitor at our bedside in a dying hour. Do you remember that place in 'Pilgrim's Progress' which describes Old Honest's passage across the river of death? 'The river,' says Bunyan, 'at that time overflowed its banks in some places; but Mr Honest, in his lifetime, had spoken to one, Good Conscience, to meet him there: the which he also did, and lent him his hand, and so helped him over.' Believe me, there is a mine of truth in that passage.

Let us hear the Apostle once more. He looks *forward* to the great day of reckoning, and he does it without doubt. Mark his words: 'henceforth there is laid up for me a crown of righteousness, which the Lord, the righteous Judge, shall give me at that day; and not to me only, but unto all them also that love his appearing.' A glorious reward, he seems to say, is ready and laid up in store for me: even that crown which is only given to the righteous. In the great day of judgment the Lord shall give this crown to me, and to all beside me who have loved him as an unseen Saviour, and longed to see him face to face. My work on earth is over. This one thing now remains for me to look forward to, and nothing more.

Reader, observe that the Apostle speaks without any hesitation or distrust. He regards the crown as a sure thing; as his own already. He declares with unfaltering confidence his firm persuasion that the righteous Judge will give it to him. Paul was no stranger to all the circumstances and accompaniments of that solemn day to which he referred. The great white throne, - the assembled world, - the open books, - the revealing of all secrets, - the listening angels, -

the awful sentence, - the eternal separation of the lost and saved, - all these were things with which he was well acquainted. But none of these things moved him. His strong faith overleaped them all, and only saw Jesus, his all-prevailing Advocate, and the blood of sprinkling, and sin washed away. 'A crown,' he says, 'is laid up for me.' 'The Lord himself *shall* give it to me.' He speaks as if he saw it all with his own eyes.

Such are the main things which these verses contain. Of most of them I cannot pretend to speak, for space would not allow me. I shall only try to set before you one point in the passage, and that is 'the assured hope' with which the Apostle looks forward to his own prospects in the day of judgment.

I shall do this the more readily, because of the great importance which I feel attaches to the subject of assurance, and the great neglect with which, I humbly conceive, it is often treated in this day.

But I shall do it at the same time with fear and trembling. I feel that I am treading on very difficult ground, and that it is easy to speak rashly and unscripturally in this matter. The road between truth and error is here especially a narrow pass, and if I shall be enabled to do good to some without doing harm to others, I shall be very thankful.

Reader, there are four things I wish to bring before you in speaking of the subject of assurance, and it may clear our way if I name them to you at once.

First, then, I will try to show you that *an assured hope, such as Paul here expresses, is a true and scriptural thing.*

Secondly, I will make this broad concession, - that a *man may never arrive at this assured hope, and yet be saved.*

Thirdly, I will give you some reasons why *an assured hope is exceedingly to be desired.*

Lastly, I will try to point out some

causes *why an assured hope is so seldom attained.*

CHAPTER 1

First, then I will try to show you that an assured hope is a true and scriptural thing.

Assurance, such as Paul expresses in the verses, which head this book, is not a mere fancy or feeling. It is not the result of high animal spirits, or a sanguine temperament of body. It is a positive gift of the Holy Ghost, bestowed without reference to men's bodily frames or constitutions, and a gift which *every believer* in Christ ought to aim at and seek after.

The Word of God appears to me to teach that a believer may arrive at an assured confidence with regard to his own salvation.

I would lay it down fully and broadly, that a true Christian, a converted man, may reach that comfortable degree of faith in Christ, that in general he shall feel entirely confident as to the pardon and safety of his soul, - shall seldom be troubled with doubts, - seldom be distracted with hesitation, - seldom be distressed by anxious questionings, - and, in short, though vexed by many an inward conflict with sin, shall look forward to death without trembling, and to judgment without dismay.

Such is my account of assurance, I will ask you to mark it well. I say neither less nor more than I have here laid down.

Now, such a statement as this is often disputed and denied. Many cannot see the truth of it at all.

The Church of Rome denounces assurance in the most unmeasured terms. The Council of Trent declares roundly, that a 'believer's assurance of the pardon of his sins is a vain and ungodly confidence'; and Cardinal Bellarmine, the well-known champion of Romanism, calls it 'a prime error of heretics'.

The vast majority of the worldly

among ourselves oppose the doctrine of assurance. It offends and annoys them to hear of it. They do not like others to feel comfortable and sure, because they never feel so themselves. That *they* cannot receive it is certainly no marvel.

But there are also some true believers who reject assurance, or shrink from it as a doctrine fraught with danger. They consider it borders on presumption. They seem to think it a proper humility never to be confident, and to live in a certain degree of doubt. This is to be regretted, and does much harm.

I frankly allow there are some *presumptuous* persons who profess to feel a confidence for which they have no Scriptural warrant. There always are some people who think well of themselves when God thinks ill, just as there are some who think ill of themselves when God thinks well. There always will be such. There never yet was a Scriptural truth without abuses and counterfeits. God's election, - man's impotence, - salvation by grace, - all are alike abused. There will be fanatics and enthusiasts as long as the world stands. But, for all this, assurance is a real, sober, and true thing; and God's children must not let themselves be driven from the use of a truth, merely because it is abused.

My answer to all who deny the

existence of real, well-grounded assurance is simply this, - What saith the Scriptures? If assurance be not there, I have not another word to say.

But does not Job say, 'I *know* that my Redeemer liveth, and that he shall stand at the latter day upon the earth: and though, after my skin, worms destroy this body, yet in my flesh shall I see God' (Job 19:25,26)?

Does not David say, 'Though I walk through the valley of the shadow of death, I will *fear no* evil: for thou art with me; thy rod and thy staff they comfort me' (Ps 23:4)?

Does not Isaiah say, 'thou wilt

keep him in *perfect peace*, whose mind is stayed on thee: because he trusteth in thee' (Is 26:3)? And again, 'The work of righteousness shall be peace; and the effect of righteousness, quietness and *assurance* for ever' (Is 32:17).

Does not Paul say to the Romans, 'I am *persuaded* that neither death, nor life, nor angels, nor principalities, nor powers, nor things present, nor things to come, nor height, nor depth, nor any other creature, shall be able to separate us from the love of God, which is in Christ Jesus our Lord' (Rom 8:38,39)?

Does he not say to the Corinthians, 'We *know* that if our earthly house of this tabernacle were dissolved, we have a building of God, an house not made with hands, eternal in the heavens' (2 Cor 5:1)?

And again, 'We are always *confident*, knowing that, whilst we are at home in the body, we are absent from the Lord' (2 Cor 5:6).

Does he not say to Timothy, 'I *know* whom I have believed, and am *persuaded* that he is able to keep that which I have committed unto him' (2 Tim 1:12)?

And does he not speak to the Colossians of 'the full assurance of understanding' (Col 2:2) and to the Hebrews of the 'full assurance of faith', and the 'full assurance of hope' (Heb 10:22; 6:11)?

Does not Peter say expressly, 'Give diligence to make your calling and election *sure*' (2 Peter 1:10)?

Does not John say, 'We *know* that we have passed from death unto life' (1 John 3:14)? And again, 'These things have I written unto you that believe on the name of the Son of God, that ye may *know* that ye have eternal life' (1 John 5:13). And again, 'We *know* that we are of God' (1 John 5:19).

Reader, what shall we say to these things? I desire to speak with all humility on any controverted point. I feel that I am only a poor fallible child of Adam myself. But I must say, that in the passages I have just quoted I see something far higher than the mere 'hopes' and 'trusts' with which so many believers appear content in this day. I see the language of persuasion, confidence, knowledge, - nay, I may also say, of certainty. And I feel, for my own part, if I may take these Scriptures in their plain, obvious meaning, *the doctrine of assurance is true*.

But my answer, furthermore, to all who dislike the doctrine of assurance, as bordering on presumption, is this: it can hardly be presumption to tread in the steps of Peter and Paul, of Job and of John. They were all eminently humble and lowly-minded men, if ever any were; and yet they all speak of their own state with an assured hope. Surely this should teach us that deep humility and strong assurance are perfectly compatible, and that there is not any necessary connection between spiritual confidence and pride.

My answer, furthermore, is, that many have attained to such an assured hope as our text expresses, even in modern times. I will not concede for a moment that it was a peculiar privilege confined to the Apostolic day. There have been, in our own land, many believers who have appeared to walk in almost uninterrupted fellowship with the Father and the Son, - who have seemed to enjoy an almost unceasing sense of the light of God's reconciled countenance shining down upon them, and have left their experience on record. I could mention well-known names, if space permitted. The thing has been, and is, - and that is enough.

My answer, lastly, is, it cannot be wrong to feel confidently in a manner where God speaks unconditionally, - to believe decidedly when God promises decidedly, - to have a sure persuasion of pardon and peace when we rest on the word and oath of him that never changes.

It is an utter mistake to suppose that the believer who feels assurance is resting on anything he sees in himself. He simply leans on the Mediator of the New Covenant, and the Scripture of truth. He believes the Lord Jesus means what he says, and *takes him at his word*. Assurance, after all, is no more than a *full-grown faith*; a masculine faith that grasps Christ's promise with both hands, - a faith that argues like the good centurion, if the Lord 'speak the word only', I am healed. Wherefore, then should I doubt (Matt 8:8)?

Reader, you may be sure that Paul was the last man in the world to build his assurance on anything of his own. He who could write himself down 'chief of sinners' (1 Tim 1:15) had a deep sense of his own guilt and corruption.

But then he had a still deeper sense of the length and breadth of Christ's righteousness imputed to him. He, who would cry, 'O wretched man that I am' (Rom 7:24), had a clear view of the fountain of evil within his heart.

But then he had a still clearer view of that other Fountain which can remove 'all sin and uncleanness'. He, who thought himself 'less than the least of all saints' (Ephes 3:8), had a lively and abiding feeling of his own weakness.

But he had a still livelier feeling that Christ's promise, 'My sheep shall never perish' (John 10:28), could not be broken. Paul knew, if ever man did, that he was a poor, frail bark, floating on a stormy ocean. He saw, if any did, the rolling waves and roaring tempest by which he was surrounded. But then he looked away from self to Jesus and was not afraid. He remembered that anchor within the veil, which is both 'sure and steadfast'. He remembered the word, and work, and constant intercession of him that loved him and gave himself for him. And this it was, and nothing else, that enabled him to say so boldly, 'A crown is laid up for me, and the Lord shall give it to me'; and to conclude so surely, 'The Lord will preserve me; I shall never be confounded.'

I may not dwell longer on this part of the subject. I think you will allow I have shown ground for the assertion I made, - that assurance is a true thing.

CHAPTER 2

A believer may never arrive at this assured hope, which Paul expresses, and yet be saved.

I grant this most freely. I do not dispute it for a moment. I would not desire to make one contrite heart sad that God has not made sad, or to discourage one fainting child of God or to leave the impression that men have no part or lot in Christ, except they feel assurance.

A person may have saving faith

in Christ, and yet never enjoy an assured hope, like the Apostle Paul. To believe and have a glimmering hope of acceptance is one thing; to have joy and peace in our believing, and abound in hope, is quite another. All God's children have faith; not all have assurance. I think this ought never to be forgotten.

I know some great and good men have held a different opinion. I believe that many excellent ministers of the Gospel, at whose feet I would gladly sit, do not allow the distinction I have stated. But I desire to call no man master. I dread as much as any one the idea of healing the wounds of conscience slightly; but I should think any other view than that I have given a most uncomfortable Gospel to preach, and one very likely to keep souls back a long time from the gate of life.

I do not shrink from saying, that by grace a man may have sufficient faith to flee to Christ; sufficient faith really to lay hold on him, really to trust in him, - really to be a child of God, - really to be saved; and yet to his last day be never free from much anxiety, doubt, and fear.

'A letter,' says an old writer, 'may be written, which is not sealed; so grace may be written in the heart, yet the Spirit may not set the seal of assurance to it.'

A child may be born heir to a great fortune, and yet never be aware of his riches; live childish, die childish, and never know the greatness of his possessions.

And so also a man may be a babe in Christ's family; think as a babe, speak as a babe; and though saved, never enjoy a lively hope, or know the real privileges of his inheritance.

Reader, do not mistake my meaning, while you hear me dwell strongly on assurance. Do not do me the injustice to say, I told you none were saved except such as could say with Paul, 'I know and am persuaded, - there is a crown laid up for me.' I do not say so. I tell you nothing of the kind.

Faith in the Lord Jesus Christ a man *must* have, beyond all question, if he is to be saved. I know no other way of access to the Father. I see no intimation of mercy, excepting through Christ. A man *must* feel his sins and lost estate, *must* come to Jesus for pardon and salvation, *must* rest his hope on him, and on him alone. But if he only has faith to do this, however weak and feeble that faith may be, I will engage, from Scripture warrants, he shall not miss heaven.

Never, never let us curtail the freeness of the glorious Gospel, or clip its fair proportions. Never let us make the gate more strait and the way more narrow than pride and love of sin have made it already.

The Lord Jesus is very pitiful and of tender mercy. He does not regard the *quantity* of faith, but the *quality*. He does not measure its degree, but its truth. He will not break any bruised reed, nor quench any smoking flax. He will never let it be said that any perished at the foot of the cross. 'Him that cometh unto me,' he says, 'I will in no wise cast out' (John 6:37).

Yes, reader: though a man's faith be no bigger than a grain of mustard seed, if it only brings him to Christ, and enables him to touch the hem of his garment, he shall be saved, - saved as surely as the oldest saint in paradise; saved as completely and eternally as Peter, or John, or Paul.

There are degrees in our sanctification. In our justification there are none. What is written, is written, and shall never fail: 'Whoseover believeth on him,' - not whosoever has a strong and mighty faith, - 'Whosoever *believeth* on him shall not be ashamed' (Rom 10:11).

But all this time, I would have you take notice, the poor soul may have no full assurance of his pardon and acceptance with God. He may be troubled with fear upon fear, and doubt upon doubt. He may have many a question and many an anxiety, - many a struggle, and many a misgiving, - clouds and darkness, - storm and tempest to the very end.

I will engage, I repeat, that bare simple faith in Christ shall save a man, though he may never attain to assurance; but I will not engage it shall bring him to heaven with strong and abounding consolations. I will engage it shall land him safe in harbour; but I will not engage he shall enter that harbour in full sail, confident and rejoicing. I shall not be surprised if he reaches his desired haven weather-beaten and tempest-tossed, scarcely realising his own safety, till he opens his eyes in glory.

Reader, I believe it is of great importance to keep in view this distinction between faith and assurance. It explains things which an inquirer in religion sometimes finds it hard to understand.

Faith, let us remember, is the root, and assurance is the flower. Doubtless you can never have the flower without the root; but it is no less certain you may have the root and not the flower.

Faith is that poor trembling woman who came behind Jesus

in the press and touched the hem of his garment (Mark 5:27). Assurance is Stephen standing calmly in the midst of his murderers, and saying, 'I see the heavens opened, and the Son of man standing on the right hand of God' (Acts 7:56).

Faith is the penitent thief, crying, 'Lord, remember me' (Luke 23:42). Assurance is Job, sitting in the dust, covered with sores, and saying, 'I know that my Redeemer liveth' (Job 19:25). 'Though he slay me, yet will I trust in him' (Job 13:15).

Faith is Peter's drowning cry as he began to sink: 'Lord, save me' (Matt 14:30). Assurance is that same Peter declaring before the

Council in after times, 'This is the stone which was set at nought of you builders, which is become the head of the corner. Neither is there salvation in any other: for there is none other name under heaven given among men, whereby we must be saved' (Acts 4:11,12).

Faith is the anxious, trembling voice, 'Lord, I believe; help thou mine unbelief' (Mark 9:24). Assurance is the confident challenge, 'Who shall lay anything to the charge of God's elect? Who is he that condemneth?' (Rom 8:33,34).

Faith is Saul praying in the house of Judas at Damascus, sorrowful, blind, and alone (Acts 9:11). Assurance is Paul, the aged prisoner, looking calmly into the grave, and saying, 'I know whom I have believed. There is a crown laid up for me' (2 Tim 1:12; 4: 8).

Faith is *life*. How great the blessing! Who can tell the gulf between life and death? And yet life may be weak, sickly, unhealthy, painful, trying, anxious, worn, burdensome, joyless, smileless to the very end.

Assurance is *more than life*. It is health, strength, power, vigour, activity, energy, manliness, beauty. Reader, it is not a question of saved or not saved that lies before us, but of privilege or no privilege. It is not a question of peace or no peace, but of great peace or little peace. It is not a question between the wanderers of this world and the school of Christ: it is one that belongs only to the school; it is between the first form and the last.

He that has faith does *well*. Happy should I be, if I thought all readers of this book had it. Blessed, thrice blessed are they that believe. They are safe. They are washed. They are justified. They are beyond the power of hell. Satan, with all his malice, shall never pluck them out of Christ's hand.

But he that has assurance does *far better*, - sees more, feels more, knows more, enjoys more, has more days like those spoken of in Deuteronomy: even 'the days of heaven upon the earth' (Deut 11:21).

CHAPTER 3

Some reasons why an assured hope is exceedingly to be desired.

I ask your attention to this point especially. I heartily wish that assurance was more sought after than it is. Too many among those who believe begin doubting and go on doubting, live doubting and die doubting, and go to heaven in a kind of mist.

It will ill become me to speak in a slighting way of 'hopes' and 'trusts'. But I fear many of us sit down content with them, and go no further. I should like to see fewer 'peradventures' in the Lord's family, and more who could say, 'I know and am persuaded'.

Oh, that all believers would covet the best gifts, and not be content with less! Many miss the full tide of blessedness the Gospel was meant to convey. Many keep themselves in a low and starved condition of soul, while their Lord is saying, 'Eat and drink abundantly, O beloved. Ask and receive that your joy may be full' (Cant 5:1; John 16:24).

1. *Let us remember, then, for one thing, that assurance is to be*

desired, because of the present comfort and peace it affords.

Doubts and fears have power to spoil much of the happiness of a true believer in Christ. Uncertainty and suspense are bad enough in any condition, - in the matter of our health, our property, our families, our affections, our earthly callings, - but never so bad as in the affairs of our souls. And so long as a believer cannot get beyond 'I hope' and 'I trust', he manifestly feels a degree of uncertainty about his spiritual state. The very words imply as much. He says, 'I hope', because he dares not say, 'I know'.

Now assurance goes far to set a

child of God free from this painful kind of bondage, and thus ministers mightily to his comfort. It enables him to feel that the great business of life is a settled business, the great debt a paid debt, the great disease a healed disease, and the great work a finished work; and all other business, diseases, debts, and works, are then by comparison small.

In this way assurance makes him patient in tribulation, calm under bereavement, unmoved in sorrow, not afraid in evil tidings, in every condition content, for it gives him a *fixedness* of heart.

It sweetens his bitter cups, it lessens the burden of his crosses, it smooths the rough places over which he travels, it lightens the valley of the shadow of death.

It makes him always feel that he has something solid beneath his feet, and something firm under his hands, - a sure friend by the way, and a sure home at the end.

Assurance will help a man to bear poverty and loss. It will teach him to say, 'I know that I have in heaven a better and more enduring substance. Silver and gold have I none, but grace and glory are mine, and these can never make themselves wings and flee away. Though the fig tree shall not blossom, yet I will rejoice in the Lord' (Habak 3:17,18).

Assurance will support a child of God under the heaviest bereavements, and assist him to feel 'It is well'. An assured soul will say, 'Though beloved ones are taken from me, yet Jesus is the same, and is alive for evermore. Though my house be not as flesh and blood could wish, yet I have an everlasting covenant, ordered in all things and sure' (2 Kings 4:26; Heb 13: 8; 2 Sam 23:5).

Assurance will enable a man to praise God, and be thankful, even in a prison, like Paul and Silas at Philippi. It can give a believer songs even in the darkest night, and joy when all things seem going against him (Job 2:10; Psa 42:8).

Assurance will enable a man to sleep with the full prospect of death on the morrow, like Peter in Herod's dungeon. It will teach him to say, 'I will both lay me down in peace and sleep; for thou, Lord, only makest me dwell in safety' (Psa 4:8).

Assurance can make a man rejoice to suffer shame for Christ's sake, as the Apostles did. It will remind him that he may 'rejoice and be exceedingly glad' (Matt 5:12), and that there is in heaven an exceeding weight of glory that shall make amends for all (2 Cor 4:17).

Assurance will enable a believer to meet a violent and painful death without fear, as Stephen did in the beginning of Christ's Church, and as Cranmer, Ridley, Latimer and Taylor did in our own land.

It will bring to his heart the texts, 'Be not afraid of them which kill the body, and after that have no more that they can do' (Luke 12:4). 'Lord Jesus, receive my spirit' (Acts 7:59).

Assurance will support a man in pain and sickness, make all his bed, smooth down his dying pillow. It will enable him to say, 'If my earthly house fail, I have a building of God' (2 Cor 5:1). 'I desire to depart, and to be with Christ' (Phil 1:23). 'My flesh and my heart may fail, but God is the strength of my heart, and my portion for ever' (Psa 73:26).

Reader, the comfort assurance can give in the hour of death is a point of great importance. Believe me, you will never think assurance so precious as when your turn comes to die.

In that awful hour, there are few believers who do not find out the value and privilege of an 'assured hope', whatever they may have thought about it during their lives. General 'hopes' and 'trusts' are all very well to live upon, while the sun shines, and the body is strong: but when you come to die, you will want to be able to say, 'I *know*' and 'I *feel*'.

Believe me, Jordan is a cold stream, and we have to cross it alone. No earthly friend can help us. The last enemy, even death, is a strong foe. When our souls are departing there is no cordial like the strong wine of assurance.

There is a beautiful expression in the Prayer-book service for the Visitation of the Sick: 'The Almighty Lord, who is a most strong tower to all them that put their trust in him, be now and evermore thy defence, and make thee *know* and *feel* that there is none other name under heaven, through whom thou mayest receive health and salvation, but only the name of our Lord Jesus Christ.'

The compilers of that service showed great wisdom there. They saw that when the eyes grow dim, and the heart grows faint, and the spirit is on the eve of departing, there must then be *knowing* and *feeling* what Christ has done for us, or else there cannot be perfect peace.

2.   *Let us remember, for another thing, that assurance is to be desired, because it tends to make a Christian an active, working Christian.*

None, generally speaking, do so much for Christ on earth as those who enjoy the fullest confidence of a free entrance into heaven. That sounds wonderful, I daresay, but it is true.

A believer who lacks an assured hope will spend much of his time in inward searchings of heart about his own state. Like a nervous, hypochondriacal person, he will be full of his own ailments, his own doubtings and questionings, his own conflicts and corruptions. In short, you will often find he is so taken up with this internal warfare that he has little leisure for other things, little time to work for God.

Now, a believer, who has, like Paul, an assured hope, is free from these harassing distractions. He does not vex his soul with doubts about his own pardon and acceptance. He looks at the everlasting covenant sealed with blood, at the finished work and never-broken word of his Lord and Saviour, and therefore counts his salvation a *settled thing*. And thus he is able to give an undivided attention to the work of the Lord, and so in the long run to do more.

Take, for an illustration of this, two English emigrants, and suppose them set down side by side in New Zealand or Australia. Give each of them a piece of land to clear and cultivate. Let the portions allotted to them be the same both in quantity and quality. Secure that land to them by every needful legal instrument; let it be conveyed as freehold to them and theirs for ever; let the conveyance be publicly registered, and the property made sure to them by every deed and security that man's ingenuity can devise.

Suppose, then, that one of them shall set to work to bring his land into cultivation, and labour at it day after day without intermission or cessation.

Suppose in the meanwhile, that the other shall be continually leaving his work, and going repeatedly to the public registry to ask whether the land really is his own, - whether there is not some mistake, - whether, after all, there is not some flaw in the legal instruments which conveyed it to him.

The one shall never doubt his

title, but just work diligently on.

The other shall hardly ever feel sure of his title, and spend half his time in going to Sydney, or Melbourne, or Auckland with needless inquiries about it.

Which, now, of these two men will have made most progress in a year's time? Who will have done the most for his land, got the greatest breadth of soil under tillage, have the best crops to show, be altogether the most prosperous?

Reader, you know as well as I do. I need not supply an answer. There can only be one reply. Undivided attention will always attain the greatest success.

It is much the same in the

matter of our title to 'mansions in the skies'. None will do so much for the Lord who bought him as the believer who sees his title clear and is not distracted by unbelieving hesitations. The joy of the Lord will be that man's strength. 'Restore unto me,' says David, 'The joy of thy salvation; *then* will I teach transgressors thy ways' (Psa 51:12, 13).

Never were there such working Christians as the Apostles. They seemed to live to labour. Christ's work was truly their meat and drink. They counted not their lives dear to themselves. They spent and were spent. They laid down ease, health, worldly comfort, at the foot of the cross. And one grand cause of this, I believe, was their assured hope. They were men who could say, 'We *know* that we are of God, and the whole world lieth in wickedness' (1 John 5:19).

3. *Let us remember, for another thing, that assurance is to be desired, because it tends to make a Christian a decided Christian.*

Indecision and doubt about our own state in God's sight is a grievous one, and the mother of many evils. It often produces a wavering and unstable walk in following the Lord. Assurance helps to cut many a knot, and to make the path of Christian duty clear and plain.

Many, of whom we feel hopes that they are God's children, and have true grace, however weak, are continually perplexed with doubts on points of practice. 'Should we do such-and-such a thing? Shall we give up this family custom? Ought we to go into that company? How shall we draw the line about visiting? What is to be the measure of our dressing and our entertainments? Are we never, under any circumstances, to dance, never to touch a card, never to attend parties of pleasure?' These are a kind of questions which seem to give them constant trouble. And often, very often, the simple root of their perplexity is, that they do not feel assured they are themselves children of God. They have not yet settled the point, which side of the gate they are on. They do not know whether they are inside the ark or not.

That a child of God ought to act in a certain decided way they quite feel, but the grand question is, 'Are they children of God themselves?' If they only felt they were so, they would go straight forward, and take a decided line. But not feeling sure about it, their conscience is for ever hesitating and coming to a deadlock. The devil whispers, 'Perhaps, after all, you are only a hypocrite: what right have you to take a decided course? Wait till you are really a Christian.' And this whisper too often turns the scale, and leads on to some miserable compromise, or wretched conformity to the world.

Reader, I believe you have here one chief reason why so many in this day are inconsistent, trimming, unsatisfactory, and half-hearted in their conduct about the world. Their faith fails. They feel no assurance that they are Christ's, and so feel a hesitancy about breaking with the world. They shrink from laying aside all the ways of the old man, because they are not quite confident they have put on the new. Depend on it, one secret cause of halting between two opinions is want of assurance. When people can say decidedly, 'The Lord he is the God', their course becomes very clear (1 Kings 18:39).

4. *Let us remember, finally, that assurance is to be desired, because it tends to make the holiest Christians*.

This, too, sounds wonderful and strange, and yet it is true. It is one of the paradoxes of the Gospel, contrary, at first sight, to reason and common sense, and yet it is a fact. Cardinal Bellarmine was seldom more wide of the truth than when he said, 'Assurance tends to carelessness and sloth'. He that is freely forgiven by Christ will always do much for Christ's glory, and he that enjoys the fullest assurance of this forgivenss will ordinarily keep up the closest walk with God. It is a faithful saying in 1 John 3:3: 'He that hath this hope in him purifieth himself, even as he is pure'. A hope that does not purify is a mockery, a delusion, and a snare.

None are so likely to maintain a watchful guard over hearts and lives as those who know the comfort of living in near communion with God. They feel their privilege, and will fear losing it. They will dread falling from their high estate, and marring their own comforts, by bringing clouds between themselves and Christ. He that goes on a journey with little money about him takes little thought of danger, and cares little how late he travels. He, on the contrary, that carries gold and jewels will be a cautious traveller. He will look well to his roads, his house, and his company, and run no risks. The fixed stars are those that tremble most. The man that most fully enjoys the light of God's reconciled countenance, will be a man tremblingly afraid of losing its blessed consolations, and jealously fearful of doing anything to grieve the Holy Ghost.

Reader, I commend these four points to your serious consideration. Would you like to feel the everlasting arms around you, and to hear the voice of Jesus daily drawing nigh to your soul, and saying, 'I am thy salvation'?

Would you like to be a useful labourer in the vineyard in your day and generation?

Would you be known of all men as a bold, firm, decided, single-eyed, uncompromising follower of Christ?

Would you be eminently spiritually-minded and holy?

I doubt not some readers will

say, 'These are the very things our hearts desire. We long for them. We pant after them: but they seem far from us.'

Now, has it never struck you that your neglect of assurance may possibly be the main secret of all your failures, that the low measure of faith which satisfies you may be the cause of your low degree of peace? Can you think it a strange thing that your graces are faint and languishing, when faith, the root and mother of them all, is allowed to remain feeble and weak?

Take my advice this day. Seek an increase of faith. Seek an assured hope of salvation like the

Apostle Paul's. Seek to obtain a simple, childlike confidence in God's promises. Seek to be able to say with Paul, 'I know whom I have believed: I am persuaded that he is mine, and I am his.'

You have very likely tried other ways and methods, and completely failed. Change your plan. Go upon another tack. Lay aside your doubts. Lean more entirely on the Lord's arm. Begin with implicit trusting. Cast aside your faithless backwardness to take the Lord at his word. Come and roll yourself, your soul, and your sins upon your gracious Saviour. Begin with simple believing, and all other things shall soon be added to you.

CHAPTER 4

I come now to the last thing of which I spoke. I promised to point out to you some probable causes why an assured hope is so seldom atttained. I will do it very shortly.

This is a very serious question, and ought to raise in all great searchings of heart. Few, certainly, of Christ's people seem to reach up to this blessed spirit of assurance. Many, comparatively, believe, but few are persuaded. Many, comparatively, have saving faith, but few that glorious confidence which shines forth in the language of St Paul. That such is the case, I think we must all allow.

Now, why is this so? - why is a thing which two Apostles have strongly enjoined us to seek after, a thing of which few believers have any experimental knowledge? Why is an assured hope so rare?

I desire to offer a few suggestions on this point, with all humility. I know that many have never attained assurance, at whose feet I would gladly sit both in earth and heaven. *Perhaps* the Lord sees something in the natural temperament of some of his children, which makes assurance not good for them. *Perhaps*, in order to be kept in spiritual health, they need to be kept very low. God only knows. Still, after every allowance, I fear there are many believers without an assured hope, whose case may too often be explained by causes such as these.

1. *One most common cause, I suspect, is a defective view of the doctrine of justification.*

I am inclined to think that justification and sanctification are insensibly confused together in the minds of many believers. They receive the gospel truth, - that there must be something done *in us*, as well as something done *for us*, if we are true members of Christ; and so far they are right. But, then, without being aware of it, perhaps, they seem to imbibe the idea that their justification is, in some degree, effected by something within themselves.

They do not clearly see that Christ's work, not their own work, - either in whole or in part, either directly or indirectly, - is the alone ground of our acceptance with God; that justification is a thing entirely without us, for which nothing whatever is needful on our part but simple faith, - and that the weakest believer is as fully and completely justified as the strongest.

Many appear to forget that we

are saved and justified as sinners, and only sinners; and that we never can attain to anything higher, if we live to the age of Methuselah. *redeemed* sinners, *justified* sinners, and *renewed* sinners doubtless we must be, - but sinners, sinners, sinners, always to the very last. They do not seem to comprehend that there is a wide difference between our justification and our sanctification.

Our justification is a perfect finished work, and admits of no degrees. Our sanctification is imperfect and incomplete, and will be till the last hour of our life. They appear to expect that a believer may at some period of his life be in a measure free from corruption, and attain to a kind of inward perfection. And not finding this angelic state of things in their own hearts, they at once conclude there must be something very wrong in their state. And so they go mourning all their days, - oppressed with fears that they have no part or lot in Christ, and refusing to be comforted.

Reader, consider this point well. If any believing soul desires assurance, and has not got it, let him ask himself, first of all, if he is quite sure he is sound in the faith, if his loins are thoroughly 'girt about with truth', and his eyes thoroughly clear in the matter of justification. He must know what it is simply to believe before he can expect to feel assured. Believe me, the old Galatian heresy is the most fertile source of error, both in doctrine and in practice. Seek clearer views of Christ, and what Christ has done for you. Happy is the man who really understands justification by faith without the deeds of the law.

2. *Another common cause of the absence of assurance is, slothfulness about growth in grace.*

I suspect many true believers hold dangerous and unscriptural views on this point: I do not of course mean intentionally, but they do hold them.

Many appear to me to think that once converted, they have little more to attend to, and that a state of salvation is a kind of easy chair, in which they may just sit still, lie back, and be happy. They seem to fancy that grace is given them that they may enjoy it, and they forget that it is given, like a talent, to be used, employed, and improved. Such persons lose sight of the many direct injunctions 'to increase, - to grow, - to abound more and more, - to add to our faith', and the like; and in this little-doing condition, this sitting-still state of mind, I never marvel that they miss assurance.

I believe it ought to be our

continual aim and desire to go forward, and our watchword at the beginning of every year should be, 'More and more' (1 Thess 4:1): more knowledge, - more faith, - more obedience, - more love.

If we have brought forth thirty-fold, we should seek to bring forth sixty, and if we have brought forth sixty, we should strive to bring forth a hundred. The will of the Lord is our sanctification, and it ought to be our will too. (Matt 13:23; 1 Thess 4:3.)

One thing, at all events, we may depend upon, - there is an insepa-rable connection between diligence and assurance.

'Give *diligence*,' says Peter, 'to

make your calling and election sure' (2 Peter 1:10).

'We desire,' says Paul, 'that every one of you do show the same *diligence* to the full assurance of hope unto the end' (Heb 6:11).

'The soul of the *diligent*,' says Solomon, 'shall be made fat' (Prov 13:4).

There is much truth in the old maxim of the Puritans: 'Faith of adherence comes by hearing, but faith of assurance comes not without *doing*.'

Reader, mark my words. Are you one of those who desire assurance, but have not got it? You will never get it without diligence, however much you may desire it.

There are no gains without pains in spiritual things, any more than in temporal. 'The soul of the sluggard desireth and hath nothing' (Prov 13:4).

3. *Another common cause of a want of assurance is, an inconsistent walk in life.*

With grief and sorrow I feel constrained to say, I fear nothing in this day more frequently prevents men attaining an assured hope than this. The stream of professing Christianity is far wider than it formerly was, and I am afraid we must admit, at the same time, it is much less deep.

Inconsistency of life is utterly

destructive of peace of conscience. The two things are incompatible. They cannot, and they will not, go together.

If you will have your besetting sins, and cannot make up your minds to give them up; if you will shrink from cutting off the right hand and plucking out the right eye, when occasion requires it, I will engage you will have no assurance.

A vacillating walk, - a backwardness to take a bold and decided line, - a readiness to conform to the world, a hesitating witness for Christ, - a lingering tone of religion, - all these make up a sure receipt for bringing a blight upon the garden of your soul.

It is vain to suppose you will feel assured and persuaded of your own pardon and acceptance with God, unless you count *all* God's commandments concerning *all* things to be right, and hate every sin, whether great or small (Psa 119:128). One Achan allowed in the camp of your heart will weaken your hands, and lay your consolations low in the dust. You must be daily sowing to the Spirit, if you are to reap the witness of the Spirit. You will not find and feel that all the Lord's ways are ways of pleasantness, unless you labour in all your ways to please the Lord.

I bless God our salvation in no

wise depends on our own works. By grace we are saved, - not by works of righteousness, - through faith, - without the deeds of the law. But I never would have any believer for a moment forget that our *sense* of salvation depends much on the manner of our living. Inconsistency will dim your eyes, and bring clouds between you and the sun. The sun is the same behind the clouds, but you will not be able to see its brightness or enjoy its warmth, and your soul will be gloomy and cold. It is in the path of well-doing that the day-spring of assurance will visit you, and shine down upon your heart.

'The secret of the Lord,' says

David, 'is with them that fear him; and he will show them his covenant' (Psa 25:14).

'To him that ordereth his conversation aright will I shew the salvation of God' (Psa 50:23).

'Great peace have they which love thy law: and nothing shall offend them' (Psa 119: 165).

'If we walk in the light, as he is in the light, we have fellowship one with another' (1 John 1:7).

'Let us not love in word, neither in tongue; but in deed and in truth. And hereby we *know* that we are of the truth, and shall assure our hearts before him' (1 John 3:18,19).

'Hereby we do *know* that we

know him, if we keep his commandments' (1 John 2:3).

Paul was a man who exercised himself to have always a conscience void of offence toward God and toward man (Acts 24:16). He could say with boldness, 'I have fought the good fight, I have kept the faith.' I do not wonder that the Lord enabled him to add with confidence, 'Henceforth there is a crown laid up for me, and the Lord shall give it me at that day.'

Reader, if any believer in the Lord Jesus desires assurance, and has not got it, let him think over this point also. Let him look at his own heart, look at his own conscience, look at his own life, look at his own ways, look at his own home. And perhaps when he has done that, he will be able to say, 'There is a *cause* why I have no assured hope.'

I leave the three matters I have just mentioned to your own private consideration. I am sure they are worth examining. May you examine them honestly. And may the Lord give you understanding in all things.

CHAPTER 5

In this chapter, let me speak first
to those readers who have not
given themselves to the Lord, who
have not yet come out from the
world, chosen the good part, and
followed Christ.

I ask you, then, to learn from
this subject *the privileges and comforts of a true Christian*.

I would not have you judge of
the Lord Jesus Christ by his people. The best of servants can give
you but a faint idea of that glorious Master. Neither would I have
you judge of the privileges of his

kingdom by the measure of comfort to which many of his people attain. Alas, we are most of us poor creatures! We come short, very short, of the blessedness we might enjoy.

But, depend upon it, there are glorious things in the city of our God, which they who have an assured hope taste, even in their life-time. There are lengths and breadths of peace and consolation there, which it has not entered into your heart to conceive. There is bread enough and to spare in our Father's house, though many of us certainly eat but little of it, and continue weak. But the fault must not be laid to our Master's charge; it is all our own.

And, after all, the weakest child of God has a mine of comforts within him, of which you know nothing. You see the conflicts and tossings of the surface of his heart, but you see not the pearls of great price which are hidden in the depths below. The feeblest member of Christ would not change conditions with you. The believer who possesses the least assurance is far better off than you are. He has a hope, however faint, but you have none at all. He has a portion that will never be taken from him, a Saviour that will never forsake him, a treasure that fadeth not away, however little he may realise it all at present. But, as for you, if you die as you are, your expectations will all perish. Oh, that you were wise! Oh, that you understood these things! Oh, that you would consider your latter end!

I feel deeply for you in these latter days of the world, if I ever did. I feel deeply for those whose treasure is all on earth, and whose hopes are all on this side the grave. Yes: when I see old kingdoms and dynasties shaking to the very foundation, - when I see, as we all saw a few years ago, kings, and princes, and rich men, and great men fleeing for their lives, and scarce knowing where to hide their heads, - when I see property dependent on public confidence melting like snow in spring, and public stocks and funds losing their value, - when I see these things I feel deeply for those who have no better portion than this world can give them, and no place in that kingdom that cannot be removed.

Take advice of a minister of Christ this very day. Seek durable riches, - a treasure that cannot be taken from you, - a city which hath lasting foundations. Do as the Apostle Paul did. Give yourself to the Lord Jesus Christ, and seek that incorruptible crown he is ready to bestow. Take his yoke upon you, and learn of him. Come away from a world which will never really satisfy you, and from sin which will bite like a serpent, if you cling to it, at last.

Come to the Lord Jesus as lowly sinners, and he will receive you, pardon you, give you his renewing Spirit, fill you with peace. This shall give you more real comfort than the world has ever done. There is a gulf in your heart which nothing but the peace of Christ can fill. Enter in and share our privileges. Come with us and sit down by our side.

Secondly, let me turn to all believers who read these pages, and speak to them a few words of brotherly counsel.

The main thing that I urge upon you is this, *if you have not got an assured hope of your own acceptance in Christ, resolve this day to seek it.* Labour for it. Strive after it. Pray for it. Give the Lord no rest till you 'know whom you have received'.

I feel, indeed, that the small amount of assurance in this day, among those who are reckoned God's children, is a shame and a reproach. 'It is a thing to be heavily bewailed,' says old Traill, 'that many Christians have lived twenty or forty years since Christ called them by his grace, yet *doubting* in their life.' Let us call to mind the earnest 'desire' Paul expresses, that 'every one' of the Hebrews should seek after full assurance; and let us endeavour by God's blessing, to roll this reproach away (Heb 6:11).

Believing reader, do you really mean to say that you have no desire to exchange hope for confidence, trust for persuasion, uncertainty for knowledge? Because weak faith will save you, will you therefore rest content with it? Because assurance is not essential to your entrance to heaven, will you therefore be satisfied without it upon earth? Alas, this is not a healthy state of soul to be in; this is not the mind of the Apostolic day! Arise at once, and go forward. Stick not at the foundations of religion: go on to perfection. Be not content with a day of small things. Never despise it in others, but never be content with it yourselves.

Believe me, assurance is worth the seeking. You forsake your own mercies when you rest content without it. The things I speak are for your peace. If it is good to be sure in earthly things, how much better is it to be sure in heavenly things. Your salvation is a fixed and certain thing. God knows it. Why should not you seek to know it too? There is nothing unscriptural in this. Paul never saw the book of life, and yet Paul says, 'I know, and am persuaded.'

Make it, then, your daily prayer that you may have an increase of faith. According to your faith will be your peace. Cultivate that blessed root more, and sooner or later, by God's blessing, you may hope to have the flower. You may not, perhaps, attain to full assurance all at once. It is good sometimes to be kept waiting. We do not value things which we get without trouble. But though it tarry, wait for it. Seek on, and expect to find.

There is one thing, however, of which I will not have you ignorant: *you must not be surprised if you have occasional doubts* after you have got assurance. You must not forget you are on earth, and not yet in heaven. You are still in the body, and have indwelling sin: the flesh will lust against the spirit to the very end. The leprosy will never be out of the walls of the old house till death takes it down.

And there is a devil, too, and a strong devil: a devil who tempted the Lord Jesus, and gave Peter a fall; and he will take care you know it. Some doubts there always will be. He that never doubts has nothing to lose. He that never fears possesses nothing truly valuable. He that is never jealous knows little of deep love. But be not discouraged: you shall be more than conquerors through him that loved you.

Finally, do not forget that assurance is a thing that *may be lost for a season*, even by the brightest Christians, unless they take care. Assurance is a most delicate plant. It needs daily, hourly watching, watering, tending, cherishing. So watch and pray the more when you have got it. As Rutherford says: 'Make much of assurance.' Be always upon your guard. When Christian slept, in Pilgrim's Progress, he lost his certificate. Keep that in mind.

David lost assurance for many months by falling into transgression. Peter lost it when he denied his Lord. Each found it again, undoubtedly, but not till after bitter tears. Spiritual darkness comes on horseback, and goes away on foot. It is upon us before we know that it is coming. It leaves us slowly, gradually, and not till after many days. It is easy to run down hill. It is hard work to climb up. So remember my caution, - when you have the joy of the Lord, watch and pray.

Above all, grieve not the Spirit. Quench not the Spirit. Vex not the Spirit. Drive him not to a distance, by tampering with small bad habits and little sins. Little jarrings between husbands and wives make unhappy homes; and petty inconsistencies, known and allowed, will bring in a strangeness between you and the Spirit.

Hear the conclusion of the whole matter.

The man who walks with God in Christ most closely will generally be kept in the greatest peace.

The believer who follows the Lord most fully will ordinarily enjoy the most assured hope, and have the clearest persuasion of his own salvation.

CHAPTER 6

EVIDENCES OF GRACE

It is written in the Bible, that 'if any man have not the Spirit of Christ, he is none of his' (Rom 8:9). This is a very solemn saying. It ought to raise in all who hear it great searchings of heart. How are you to know whether you have the Holy Spirit? What are the evidences by which a man may discern the grace of the Holy Spirit in his own heart?

The presence of the Holy Ghost in a man's heart can only be

known by the fruits and effects he produces. Mysterious and invisible to mortal eye as his operations are, they always lead to certain visible and tangible results. Just as you know the compass-needle to be magnetized, by its turning to the north, - just as you know there is life in a tree, by its sap, buds, leaves, and fruits, - just as you know there is a steersman on board a ship, by its keeping a steady regular course, - just so you may know the Spirit to be in a man's heart, by the influence he exercises over his thoughts, affections, opinions, habits, and life. I lay this down broadly and unhesitatingly. I find no safe ground to occupy, excepting this. I see no safeguard against the wildest enthusiasm, excepting in this position. And I see it clearly marked out in our Lord Jesus Christ's words, - 'Every tree is known by his own fruit' (Luke 6:44).

But what are the specific fruits by which the presence of the Spirit in the heart may be known? I find no difficulty in answering that question. The Holy Ghost always works after a certain definite pattern. His work is the work of a Master. The world may see no beauty in it. It is foolishness to the natural man. But 'he that is spiritual discerneth all things' (1 Cor 2:14). A well-instructed Christian knows well the fruits of the Spirit of God. Let me briefly set them before you in order. They are all clear and unmistakeable, 'plain to him that understandeth, and right to them that find knowledge' (Prov 8:9).

1. Where the Holy Ghost is, there will be *deep conviction of sin, and true repentance for it*. It is his special office to convince of sin (John 16:8). He shows the exceeding holiness of God. He teaches the exceeding corruption and infirmity of our nature. He strips us of our blind self-righteousness. He opens our eyes to our awful guilt, folly, and danger. He fills the heart with sorrow, con-

trition, and abhorrence for sin, as the abominable thing which God hateth. He that knows nothing of all this, and saunters carelessly through life, indifferent and unconcerned about his soul, is a dead man before God. He has not the Spirit of Christ!

2. Where the Holy Ghost is, there will be *lively faith in Jesus Christ* as the only Saviour. It is his special office to testify of Christ, to take of the things of Christ and show them to man (John 15:26). He leads the soul which feels its sins to Jesus and the atonement made by his blood. He shows the soul that Christ has suffered for

sin, the just for the unjust, to bring us to God. He points out to the sin-sick soul that we have only to receive Christ, believe in Christ, commit ourselves to Christ, - and pardon, peace and life eternal are at once our own. He makes us see a beautiful fitness in Christ's finished work of redemption to meet our spiritual necessities. He makes us willing to disclaim all merit of our own, and to venture all on Jesus, - looking to nothing, resting on nothing, trusting in nothing but Christ, - Christ, - Christ, - delivered for our offences, and raised again for our justification. He that knows nothing of all this, and builds on any other foundation, is dead before God. He has not the Spirit of Christ!

3. Where the Holy Ghost is, there will always be *holiness of life and conversation*. He is the Spirit of Holiness (Rom 1:4). He is the sanctifying Spirit. He takes away the hard, carnal, worldly heart of man, and puts in its place a tender, conscientious, spiritual heart, delighting in the law of God. He makes a man turn his face towards God, and desire above all things to please him, and turn his back on the fashion of this world, and no longer make that fashion his god. He sows in a man's heart the blessed seeds of love, joy, meek-

ness, longsuffering, gentleness, goodness, faith, temperance, and causes these seeds to spring up, and bear pleasant fruit. He that lacketh these things, and knows nothing of daily practical godliness, is dead before God. He has not the Spirit of Christ!

4. Where the Holy Ghost is, there will always be *the habit of earnest private prayer*. He is the Spirit of Grace and Supplication (Zech 12:10). He works in the heart as the Spirit of Adoption, whereby we cry, 'Abba, Father'. He makes a man feel that he must cry to God, and speak to God, - feebly, falteringly, weakly, it

may be, but cry he must about his soul. He makes it as natural to a man to pray as it is to an infant to breathe, with this one difference, that the infant breathes without an effort, and the new-born soul prays with much conflict and strife. He that knows nothing of real, living, fervent private prayer, and is content with some old form, or with no prayer at all, is dead before God. He has not the Spirit of Christ!

5. Finally, where the Holy Ghost is, there will always be *love and reverence for God's Word*. He makes the new-born soul desire the sincere milk of the Word, just

as the infant desires its natural food. He makes it 'delight in the law of the Lord' (1 Peter 2:2; Psa 1:2). He shows man a fulness, and depth, and wisdom, and sufficiency in the holy Scripture, which is utterly hid from the natural man's eyes. He draws him to the Word with an irresistible force, as the light and lantern, and manna, and sword, which are essential to a safe journey through this world. If the man cannot read, he makes him love to hear. If he cannot hear, he makes him love to meditate. But to the Word the Spirit always leads him. He that sees no special beauty in God's Bible, and takes no pleasure in reading, hearing, and understanding it, is dead before God. He has not the Spirit of Christ!

Reader, I place these five grand marks of the Spirit's presence before you, and confidently claim your attention to them. I believe they will bear inspection. I am not afraid of their being searched, criticised, and cross-examined. Repentance towards God, - faith toward our Lord Jesus Christ, - holiness of heart and life, - habits of real private prayer, - love and reverence towards God's Word, - these are the real proofs of the indwelling of the Holy Ghost in a man's soul. Where he is, these marks will be seen. Where he is not, these marks will be lacking.

I grant you freely that the leadings of the Spirit are not always uniform. The paths over which he conducts souls are not always one and the same. The experience that true Christians pass through in their beginnings is often very various. This only I maintain, that the *final results* the Spirit at length produces are always alike.

CHAPTER 7

Extracts from English divines, showing that there is a difference between faith and assurance, - that a believer may be justified and accepted with God, and yet not enjoy a comfortable knowledge and persuasion of his own safety, - and that the weakest faith in Christ, if it be true, will save a man as surely as the strongest.

1. Is it not necessary to justification to be assured that my sins are pardoned, and that I am justified?

No: that is no act of faith as it justifieth, but an effect and fruit that followeth after justification.

It is one thing for a man to have his salvation certain, another thing to be certain that it is certain.

Even as a man fallen into a river, and like to be drowned, as he is carried down with the flood, espies the bough of a tree hanging over the river, which he catcheth at, and clings unto with all his might to save him, and seeing no other way of succour but that, ventures his life upon it. This man, so soon as he has fastened on this bough, is in a safe condition, though all troubles, fears and terrors are not presently out of his mind, until he comes to himself, and sees himself quite out of danger. Then he is sure he is safe, but he was safe before he was sure.

Even so it is with a believer. Faith is but the espying of Christ as the only means to save, and the reaching out of the heart to lay hold upon him. God hath spoke the word, and made the promise to his Son: I believe him to be the only Saviour, and remit my soul to him to be saved by his mediation. So soon as the soul can do this, God imputeth the righteousness of his Son unto it, and it is actually justified in the court of heaven, though it is not presently quieted and pacified in the court of conscience. That is done afterwards: in some sooner, in some later, by the fruits and effects of justification. - *Archbishop Usher's Body of Divinity, 1670.*

2 There are those who doubt, because they doubt and multiply distrust upon itself, concluding that they have no faith, because they find so much and so frequent doubting within them. But this is a great mistake. Some doubtings there may be, where there is even much faith; and a little faith there may be, where there is much doubting.

Our Saviour requires, and delights in a strong, firm believing on him, though the least and weakest he rejects not. - *Archbishop Leighton's Lectures on the first nine chapters of St Matthew's Gospel. 1670.*

3. The mercy of God is greater than all the sins in the world. But we sometimes are in such a case that we think we have no faith at all; or if we have any, it is very feeble and weak. And, therefore, these are two things; to have faith, and have the feeling of faith. For some men would fain have the feeling of faith, but they cannot attain unto it; and yet they must not despair, but go forward in calling upon God, and it will come

at the length: God will open their hearts, and let them feel his goodness - *Bishop Latimer's Sermons. 1552.*

4. I know, thou sayest, that Jesus Christ came into the world to save sinners; and that 'Whosoever believeth on him shall not perish, but have eternal life' (John 3:15). Neither can I know but that, in a sense of my own sinful condition, I do cast myself in some measure upon my Saviour, and lay some hold upon his all-sufficient redemption: but, alas, my apprehensions of him are so feeble, as that they can afford no sound comfort to my soul!

Courage, my son. Were it that thou lookedst to be justified, and saved by the power of the very act of thy faith, thou hadst reason to be disheartened with the conscience of the weakness thereof; but now that the virtue and efficacy of this happy work is in the object apprehended by thee, which is the infinite merits and mercy of thy God and Saviour, which cannot be abated by thine infirmities, thou hast cause to take heart to thyself, and cheerfully to expect his salvation.

Understand thy case aright. Here is a double hand, that helps us up toward heaven. Our hand of faith lays hold upon our

Saviour; our Saviour's hand of mercy and plenteous redemption lays hold on us. Our hold of him is feeble and easily loosed; his hold of us is strong and irresistible.

If work were stood upon, a strength of hand were necessary; but now that only taking and receiving of a precious gift is required, why may not a weak hand do that as well as a strong? As well, though not as forcibly. - *Bishop Hall's Balm of Gilead. 1650.*

5. Many formerly, and those of the highest remark and eminency, have placed true faith in no lower degree than assurance, or the secure persuasion of the pardon of their sins, the acceptance of their

persons, and their future salvation.

But this, as it is very sad and uncomfortable for thousands of doubting and deserted souls, concluding all those to fall short of grace who fall short of certainty, so hath it given the Papists too great advantage.

Faith is not assurance. But this doth sometimes crown and reward a strong, vigorous and heroic faith; the Spirit of God breaking in upon the soul with an evidencing light, and scattering all that darkness and those fears and doubts which before beclouded it. -*Bishop Hopkins on the Covenants. 1680.*

6. If any persons abroad have thought that a special and full persuasion of the pardon of their sin was of the essence of faith, let them answer for it. Our divines at home generally are of another judgment. Bishop Davenant and Bishop Prideaux, and others, have shown the great difference between recumbence and assurance, and they all do account and call assurance a daughter, fruit, and consequent of faith. And the late learned Arrowsmith tell us that God seldom bestows assurance upon believers till they are grown in grace: for, says he, there is the same difference between faith of recumbence and faith of

assurance, as is between reason and learning. Reason is the foundation of learning; so, as there can be no learning if reason be wanting (as in beasts), in like manner there can be no assurance where there is no faith of adherence. Again: as reason well exercised in the study of arts and sciences arises to learning, so faith, being well exercised on its proper object, and by its proper fruits, arises to assurance. Further, as by negligence, non-attendance, or some violent disease, learning may be lost, while reason doth abide; so, by temptation, or by spiritual sloth, assurance may be lost, while saving faith may abide. Lastly, as all men have reason, but all men are not learned; so all regenerate persons have faith to comply savingly with the gospel method of salvation, but all true believers have not assurance. - *Sermon by R Fairclough, Fellow of Emmanuel College, Cambridge, in the Morning Exercises, preached at Southwark. 1660.*

7. Weak faith may fail in the applying, or in the apprehension and appropriating of Christ's benefits to a man's own self. This is to be seen in ordinary experience. For many a man there is of humble and contrite heart, that serveth God in spirit and truth, yet is not

able to say, without great doubtings and waverings, I know and am fully assured that my sins are pardoned. Now shall we say that all such are without faith? God forbid.

This weak faith will as truly apprehend God's merciful promises for the pardon of sin as strong faith, though not so soundly. Even as a man with a palsied hand can stretch it out as well to receive a gift at the hand of a king as he that is more sound, though it may be not so firmly and steadfastly. - *Exposition of the Creed, by William Perkins, Minister of Christ in the University of Cambridge. 1612.*

8. A want of assurance is not unbelief. Drooping spirits may be believers. There is a manifest distinction made between faith in Christ and the comfort of that faith, - between believing to eternal life and knowing we have eternal life. There is a difference between a child's having a right to an estate and his full knowledge of the title.

'The character of faith may be written in the heart, as letters engraven upon a seal, yet filled with so much dust as not to be distinguished. The dust hinders the reading of the letters, yet doth not raze them out. - *Discourses by Stephen Charnock, of Emmanuel Collge, Cambridge. 1680.*

9. This certainty of our salvation, spoken of by Paul, rehearsed by Peter, and mentioned by David (Psa 4:7), is that special fruit of faith which breedeth spiritual joy, and inward peace which passeth all understanding. True it is, all God's children have it not. One thing is the tree, and another thing is the fruit of the tree: one thing is faith, and another thing is the fruit of faith. And that remnant of God's elect which feel the want of this faith have, notwithstanding, faith. - *Sermons by Richard Greenham, Minister and Preacher of the Word of God. 1612.*

10. You that can clear this to your

own hearts that you have faith, though it be weak, be not discouraged, be not troubled. Consider that the smallest degree of faith is true, is saving faith as well as the greatest. A spark of fire is as true fire as any in the element of fire. A drop of water is as true water as any is in the ocean. So the least grain of faith is as true faith, and as saving as the greatest faith in the world.

The least bud draws sap from the root as well as the greatest bough. So the weakest measure of faith doth as truly ingraft thee into Christ, and by that draw life from Christ, as well as the strongest. The weakest faith hath communion with the merits and blood of Christ as well as the strongest.

The least faith marries the soul to Christ. The weakest faith hath as equal a share in God's love as the strongest. We are beloved in Christ, and the least measure of faith makes us members of Christ. The least faith hath equal right to the promises as the strongest. And, therefore, let not our souls be discouraged for weakness. - *Nature and Royalties of Faith, by Samuel Bolton DD, of Christ's College, Cambridge. 1657.*

11. A man may be in the favour of God, in the state of grace, a

justified man before God, and yet want the sensible assurance of his salvation, and of the favour of God in Christ.

A man may have saving grace in him, and not perceive it himself; a man may have true justifying faith in him, and not have the use and operation of it, so far as to work in him a comfortable assurance of his reconciliation with God. Nay, I will say more: a man may be in the state of grace, and have true justifying faith in him, and yet be so far from sensible assurance of it in himself, as in his own sense and feeling he may seem to be assured of the contrary. Job was certainly in this case when he cried unto God, 'Wherefore hidest thou thy face, and holdest me for thine enemy? (Job 13:24).

The weakest faith will justify. If thou canst receive Christ and rest upon him, even with the weakest faith, it will serve thy turn. - Take heed thou think not it is the strength of thy faith that justifieth thee. No, no: it is Christ and his perfect righteousness which thy faith receiveth and resteth upon it that doth it. He that hath the feeblest and weakest hand may receive an alms, and apply a sovereign plaster to his wound, as well as he that hath the strongest, and receive as much good by it too. - *Lectures upon the fifty-first Psalm, preached at Ashby-de-la-Zouch, by Arthur Hildersam, Minister of Jesus Christ. 1642.*

12. There are some who are true believers and yet weak in faith. They do indeed receive Christ and free grace, but it is with a shaking hand. They have, as divines say, the faith of adherence: they will stick to Christ, as theirs; but they want the faith of evidence, - they cannot see themselves as his. They are believers but of little faith. They hope that Christ will not cast them off, but are not sure that he will take them up. - *Sips of Sweetness, or Consolation for Weak Believers, by John Durant, Preacher in*

13. The act of faith is to apply Christ to the soul; and this the weakest faith can do as well as the strongest, if it be true. A child can hold a staff as well, though not so strongly, as a man. The prisoner through a hole sees the sun, though not so perfectly as they see in the open air. They that saw the brazen serpent, though a great way off, yet were healed.

The least faith is as precious to the believer's soul as Peter's or Paul's faith was to themselves, for it lays hold upon Christ and brings eternal salvation. -*An Exposition of the Second Epistle General of*

Peter, by the Rev Thomas Adams, Rector of St Gregory's, London. 1633.

14. Many of God's dear children for a long time may remain very doubtful as to their present and eternal condition, and know not what to conclude, whether they shall be damned, or whether they shall be saved. There are believers of several growths in the Church of God, - fathers, young men, children and babes; and as in most families there are more babes and children than grown men, so in the Church of God there are more weak, doubting Christians than strong ones, grown up to a full assurance. A babe may be

born, and yet not know it; so a man may be born again, and yet not be sure of it.

We make a difference betwixt saving faith, as such, and a full persuasion of the heart. Some of those that shall be saved may not be certain that they shall be saved; for the promise is made to the grace of faith, and not to the evidence of it, to faith as true, and not to faith as strong. They may be sure of heaven, and yet in their own sense not assured of heaven. - *Sermon by Rev Thomas Doolittle, of Pembroke Hall, Cambridge, and sometime Rector of St Alphage, London, in the Morning Exercises, at Cripplegate. 1661.*

15. I find not salvation put upon the strength of faith, but the truth of faith; not upon the brightest degree, but upon any degree of faith. It is not said, If you have such a degree of faith you shall be justified and saved; but simply believing is required. The lowest degree of true faith will do it; as Romans 10:9: 'If thou shalt confess with thy mouth the Lord Jesus, and shalt believe in thine heart that God hath raised him from the dead, thou shalt be saved.' The thief upon the cross hath not attained to such high degrees of faith: he by one act, and that of a weak faith, was justified and saved (Luke 23:42). -

Exposition of the Prophet Ezekiel, by William Greenhill, Rector of Stepney, London, and Chaplain to the Dukes of York and Gloucester. 1650.

16. Weak faith is true faith, - as precious, though not so great, as strong faith, - the same Holy Ghost the Author, the same Gospel the instrument.

If it never proves great, yet weak faith shall save, for it interests us in Christ, and makes him and all his benefits ours. For it is not the strength of our faith that saves, but truth of our faith; nor weakness of our faith that condemns, but the want of faith, - for the least faith layeth hold on Christ and so will save us. Neither are we saved by the worth or quantity of our faith, but by Christ, who is laid hold on by a weak faith as well as a strong. Just as a weak hand that can put meat into the mouth, shall feed and nourish the body as well as if it were a strong hand; seeing the body is not nourished by the strength of the hand, but by the goodness of the meat. - *The Doctrine of Faith, by John Rogers, Preacher of God's Word at Dedham, in Essex. 1634.*

17. Though your grace be never so weak, yet if ye have truth of grace, you have as great a share

in the righteousness of Christ for your justification as the strong Christian hath. You have as much of Christ imputed to you as any other. - *Sermons by William Bridge, formerly Fellow of Emmanuel College, Cambridge, and Pastor of the Church of Christ, in Great Yarmouth. 1648.*

18. It is confessed weak faith hath as much peace with God, through Christ, as another hath by strong faith, but not so much bosom peace.

Weak faith will as surely land the Christian in heaven as strong faith, for it is impossible the least dram of true grace should perish, being all incorruptible seed; but the weak, doubting Christian is not like to have so pleasant a voyage thither as another with strong faith. Though all in the ship come safe to shore, yet he that is all the way sea-sick hath not comfortable a voyage as he that is strong and healthful. - *The Christian in Complete Armour, by William Gurnell, sometime Minister at Lavenham, Suffolk. 1680.*

19. A man may have true grace that hath not the assurance of the love and favour of God, or the remission of his sins, and salvation of his soul. A man may be God's and yet he not know it; his estate

may be good, and yet he not see it; he may be in a safe condition, when he is not in a comfortable position. All may be well with him in the court of glory, when he would give a thousand worlds that all were but well in the court of conscience.

Assurance is requisite to the well-being of a Christian, but not to the being; it is requisite to the consolation of a Christian, but not to the salvation of a Christian; it is requisite to the well-being of grace, but not the mere being of grace. Though a man cannot be saved without faith, yet he may be saved without assurance. God hath in many places of the Scripture declared that without faith there is no salvation; but God hath not in any one place of Scripture declared that without assurance there is no salvation. - *Heaven on Earth, by Thomas Brooks, Preacher of the Gospel at St Margaret's, Fish Street Hill, London. 1654.*

20. We must distinguish between weakness of faith and nullity. A weak faith is true. The bruised reed is but weak, yet it is such as Christ will not break. Though thy faith be but weak, yet be not discouraged. A weak faith may receive a strong Christ: a weak hand can tie the knot in marriage

as well as a strong: a weak eye might have seen the brazen serpent. The promise is not made to strong faith, but to true. The promise doth not say, Whosoever hath a giant faith that can remove mountains, that can stop the mouth of lions, shall be saved; but whosoever believes, be his faith never so small.

You may have the water of the Spirit poured on you in sanctification, though not the oil of gladness in assurance; there may be faith of adherence, and not of evidence; there may be life in the root where there is no fruit in the branches, and faith in the heart where no fruit of assurance. - A *Body of*

Divinity, by Thomas Watson, formerly Minister of St Stephen's, Walbrook, London. 1660.

21. There is a weak faith, which yet is true, and although it be weak, yet, because it is true, it shall not be rejected of Christ.

Faith is not created perfect at the first, as Adam was, but is like a man in the ordinary course of nature, who is first an infant, then a child, then a youth, then a man.

Some utterly reject all weak ones, and tax all weakness in faith with hypocrisy. Certainly these are either proud or cruel men.

Some comfort and establish those who are weak, saying, Be

quiet: thou hast faith and grace enough and art good enough; thou needest no more, neither must thou be too righteous (Eccles 7:16). These are soft, but not safe cusions; these are fawning flatterers, and not faithful friends.

Some comfort and exhort, saying, Be of good cheer: he who hath begun a good work will also finish it in you; therefore pray that his grace may abound in you; yea, do not sit still, but go forward, and march on in the way of the Lord' (Heb 6:1). Now this is the safest and best course. - *Questions, Observations etc, upon the Gospel according to St Matthew, by Richard Ward, sometime*

Student at Cambridge, and Preacher of the Gospel in London. 1640.

22. Be not discouraged if it doth not yet appear to you that you were given by the Father to the Son. It may be, though you do not see it. Many of the given do not for a long time know it; yea, I see no great danger in saying that not a few of the given to the Son may be in darkness, and doubts and fears about it, till the last and brightest day declares it, and till the last sentence proclaims it.

If therefore any of you be in the dark about your own election, be not discouraged; it may be, though you do not know it. - *Sermon on the Lord's Prayer, by Robert Traill, Minister of the Gospel in London, and sometime at Cranbrook, Kent. 1690.*

23. Some rob themselves of their own comfort by placing saving faith in full assurance. Faith, and sense of faith, are two distinct and separables mercies; you may have truly received Christ, and not receive the knowledge or assurance of it. Some there be that say, Thou art our God, of whom God never said, You are my people; these have no authority to be called the sons of God: others there are of whom God saith, These are my

people, yet they dare not call God, their God; these have authority to be called the sons of God, yet know it not. They have received Christ, that is their safety; but they have not received the knowledge and assurance of it, that is their trouble. The father owns his child in the cradle, who yet knows him not to be his father. - *Method of grace, by John Flavel, Minister of the Gospel at Dartmouth, Devon. 1680.*

24. The faith necessary and sufficient for our salvation is not assurance. Its tendency, doubtless, is to produce that lively expectation of the Divine favour

which will issue in a full confidence. But the confidence is not itself the faith of which we speak, nor is it necessarily included in it: nay, it is a totally distinct thing.

Assurance will generally accompany a high degree of faith. But there are sincere persons who are endued with only small measures of grace, or in whom the exercise of that grace may be greatly obstructed. When such defects or hindrances prevail, many fears and distresses may be expected to rise. - *The Christian System, by the Rev Thomas Robinson, Vicar of St Mary's, Leicester. 1795.*

25. Assurance is not essential to

the being of faith. It is a strong faith; but we read likewise of a weak faith, little faith, faith like a grain of mustard seed. True saving faith in Jesus Christ is only distinguishable by its different degrees; but in every every degree, and in every subject, it is universally of the same kind. - *Sermons, by the Rev John Newton, sometime Vicar of Olney, and Rector of St Mary's, Woolnoth, London. 1767.*

26. There is no reason why weak belivers should conclude against themselves. Weak faith unites as really with Christ as strong faith, - as the least bud in the vine is drawing sap and life from the root,

no less than the strongest branch. Weak believers, therefore, have abundant cause to be grateful; and while they reach after growth in grace, ought not to overlook what they have already received.
- *Letter of Rev Henry Venn. 1784.*

27. Salvation, and the joy of salvation, are not always contemporaneous; the latter does not always accompany the former in present experience.

A sick man may be under the process of recovery and yet be in doubt concerning the restoration of his health. Pain and weakness may cause him to hesitate. A child may be heir to his estate or kingdom, and yet derive no joy from the prospect of his future inheritance. He may be unable to trace his genealogy, or to read his title-deeds, and the testament of his father; or with a capacity of reading them he may be unable to understand their import, and his guardian may for a time deem it right to suffer him to remain in ignorance. But his ignorance does not affect the validity of his title.

Personal assurance of salvation is not necessarily connected with faith. They are not essentially the same. Every believer *might* indeed infer, from the effect produced in his own heart, his own safety and privileges; but many who truly believe are unskilful in the word of righteousness, and fail of drawing the conclusion from Scriptural premises which they would be justified in drawing. - *Lectures on the Fifty-first Psalm. by the Rev Thomas Biddulph, Minister of St James', Bristol. 1830.*